# America

## A Patriotic Primer

# America

## A Patriotic Primer

LYNNE CHENEY

*Illustrated by*

ROBIN PREISS GLASSER

SIMON & SCHUSTER BOOKS FOR YOUNG READERS
NEW YORK   LONDON   TORONTO   SYDNEY   SINGAPORE

# ACKNOWLEDGMENTS

My first thanks are to Robin Preiss Glasser, whose imagination and talent have so enriched this book. I would also like to thank Stephanie Lundberg, my intelligent and efficient research assistant, for the help she has given me, and Jacqueline Preiss Weitzman, who has been smart and tireless in unearthing information for Robin.

My colleagues at the American Enterprise Institute warrant special acknowledgment. All of them together create a rich intellectual environment in which all kinds of ideas thrive, even an idea for a children's book. I'd like particularly to recognize Walter Berns for the inspiration he has provided on the subject of patriotism; Robert Goldwin for his profound knowledge, so willingly shared, of the founding period; and Chris DeMuth, president of the American Enterprise Institute, for his constant encouragement.

This book has benefited mightily from Brenda Bowen and Lee Wade, its gifted editor and designer at Simon and Schuster. And last but not least, Robert Barnett, my agent on this book, deserves much thanks for bringing us all together.
                                                                        —L. C.

SIMON & SCHUSTER BOOKS FOR YOUNG READERS
An imprint of Simon & Schuster Children's Publishing Division
1230 Avenue of the Americas
New York, New York 10020
Text copyright © 2002 by Lynne V. Cheney
Illustrations copyright © 2002
by Robin Preiss Glasser
All rights reserved, including the right of reproduction
in whole or in part in any form.
SIMON & SCHUSTER BOOKS FOR YOUNG READERS is a
trademark of Simon & Schuster.
Book design by Lee Wade
The text for this book is set in Celestia Antique.
The illustrations for this book are rendered in
black ink, watercolor washes, and colored pencils.
Printed in the United States of America

10 9 8 7 6 5 4 3 2 1
Library of Congress Cataloging-in-Publication Data
Cheney, Lynne V.
America : a patriotic primer / Lynne Cheney ; illustrated by
Robin Preiss Glasser.
p. cm.
Summary: Each letter of the alphabet is represented by
important people, ideas, and events in the history of
the United States.
ISBN 0-689-85192-8
1. United States—History—Juvenile literature. 2. United
States—Politics and government—Juvenile literature. 3. English
language—Alphabet—Juvenile literature. [1. United States—
History. 2. Alphabet.] I. Preiss-Glasser, Robin, ill. II. Title.
E178.3.C49 2002 973—dc21 2001057663
First Edition

The author wishes to thank Joe Rosenthal, whose famous photograph of the flag raising at Iwo Jima was the inspiration for the cover image of *America*, and for the picture on page 30.

The drawn image of Martha Graham on page 25 is based on Barbara Morgan's copyrighted photo, *Letter to the World* (kick), 1940, copyright © Barbara Morgan, Barbara Morgan Archives, and is used by permission.

Mrs. Cheney is donating her net proceeds from this book to the American Red Cross and to projects that foster appreciation of American history.

Simon & Schuster will donate a portion of its profits from the sale of this book to organizations that promote childhood literacy in America.

**Editor's Note:** Archaic spelling, capitalization, and punctuation in historical quotations have been modernized throughout the text.

To Kate, Elizabeth, and Grace
—L. C.

To my mother, Marcia Preiss,
who continues to inspire me
—R. P. G.

AND TO AMERICA'S CHILDREN

We live in a land of shining cities and natural splendors, a beautiful land made more beautiful still by our commitment to freedom. I wrote this book because I want my grandchildren to understand how blessed we are. I want them to know they are part of a nation whose citizens enjoy liberty and opportunity such as have never been known before. Generations have passed from the earth never dreaming that people could be as fortunate as we Americans are.

I want my granddaughters to know that, and I want them to love this country. Their parents want this for them too, and so what they do, and what the Vice President and I do, is teach them about the United States, about its geography and its people and its history. We believe, all of us, that the story of this country is its highest recommendation. Few tales are more wondrous than that of the founders of this country seeking independence and—against the odds—winning it. Few plots are more thrilling than their deciding to establish a representative form of government and—against the odds—succeeding. And few stories are more heartening than the way that the idea of equality, which was the basis for their actions, has expanded over the subsequent two centuries, including more and ever more of us in the phrase "we the people."

I hope that parents and grandparents will use this book to teach children about Washington's character, Jefferson's intellect, and Madison's wide-ranging knowledge. The upcoming generation should know about these men and their thoughts and aspirations. They should also know about the courage of Frederick Douglass, the determination of Elizabeth Cady Stanton and Susan B. Anthony, and the impassioned leadership of Martin Luther King Jr. Our children should realize that these men and women made us a better country.

We have benefited from the freedom we have enjoyed, and so has all of humankind.

As Abraham Lincoln described it, this realization was one of the reasons that Henry Clay, a luminary of American political life before the Civil War, was so deeply patriotic. Clay "loved his country," Lincoln said, "partly because it was his own country, but mostly because it was a free country; and he burned with a zeal for its advancement, prosperity and glory, because he saw in such, the advancement, prosperity and glory of human liberty, human right and human nature."

Our children should also know that you do not have to be born in this country to be an American. People born elsewhere can become citizens by taking an oath promising that they will be faithful to the Constitution, the plan of government that makes it possible for us to live in freedom. And then when they have taken the oath, they pledge allegiance to the flag and to the republic for which it stands, one nation under God, indivisible, with liberty and justice for all. By committing themselves to our founding principles, people from all around the world become part of "we the people," an equal part because the principles now apply to them.

Mary Antin, who at the end of the nineteenth century came to this country from Russia as a child, described in a book the ongoing amazement she felt at having become an American. One day, she wrote, she learned about George Washington, and suddenly she realized, "I was more nobly related than I had ever supposed. . . . George Washington, who died long before I was born, was like a king in greatness, and he and I were fellow citizens."

Mary Antin's book is called *The Promised Land,* and there are many reasons that so many people from so many countries have looked on the United States in this way. We should all commit ourselves to seeing that the children of this blessed country understand these reasons from their youngest years.

*Lynne Cheney*

A is for *America*, the land that we love.

"I lift my lamp
beside the golden door!"
—Emma Lazarus

O beautiful for patriot dream that sees beyond the years
Thine alabaster cities gleam undimmed by human tears!

# B

B is for the *Birthday* of this nation of ours.

On America's birthday there ought to be "pomp and parade," John Adams, our second president, wrote to his wife, Abigail, and "illuminations from one end of this continent to the other from this time forward forever more."

# C is for the Constitution that binds us together.

The Constitution has been the framework for our government for more than two hundred years.

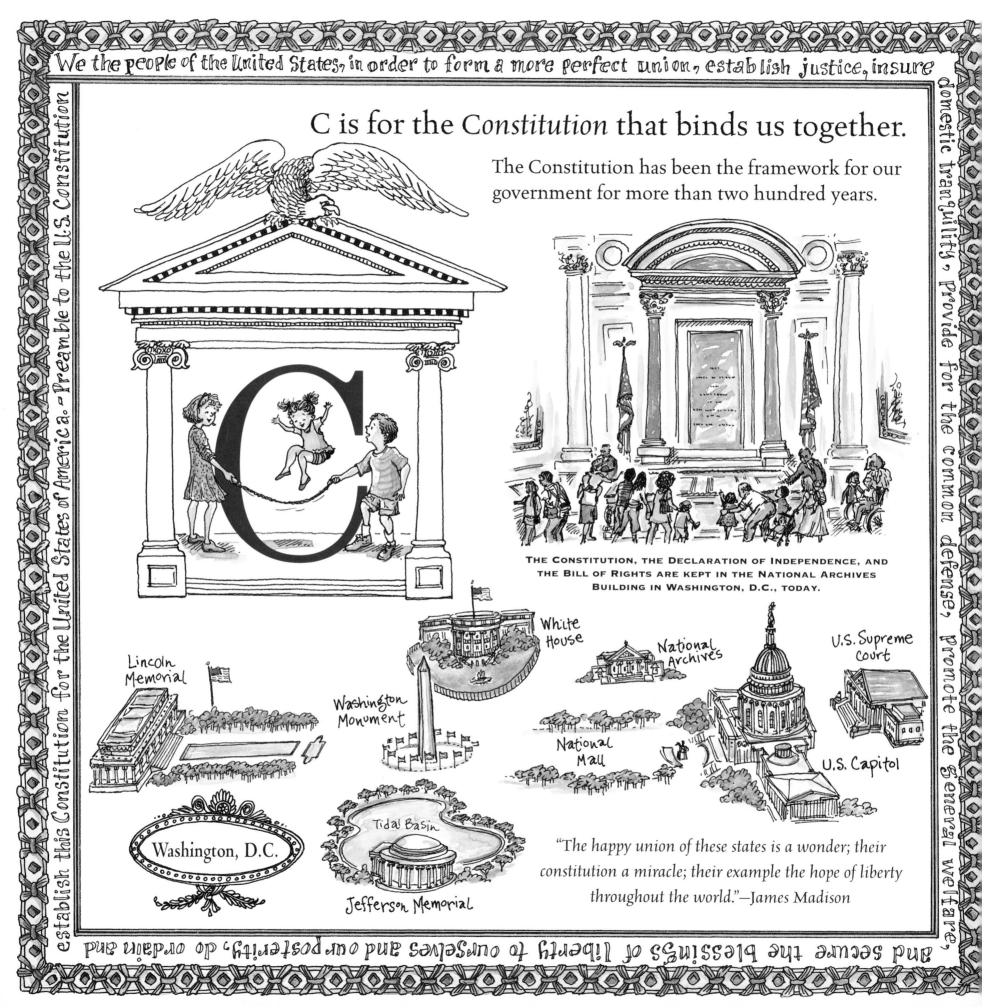

**THE CONSTITUTION, THE DECLARATION OF INDEPENDENCE, AND THE BILL OF RIGHTS ARE KEPT IN THE NATIONAL ARCHIVES BUILDING IN WASHINGTON, D.C., TODAY.**

Lincoln Memorial

White House

Washington Monument

National Archives

National Mall

U.S. Supreme Court

U.S. Capitol

Washington, D.C.

Tidal Basin

Jefferson Memorial

*"The happy union of these states is a wonder; their constitution a miracle; their example the hope of liberty throughout the world."*—James Madison

"We have it in our power to begin the world over again." ~Thomas Paine

D is for the *Declaration* that proclaimed we were free.

The Declaration of Independence, adopted on July 4, 1776, in Philadephia, Pennsylvania, declared us to be a free and independent nation.

JOHN HANCOCK WAS THE FIRST TO SIGN THE DECLARATION. HE WROTE HIS NAME LARGE BECAUSE, SOME SAY, HE WANTED TO BE SURE THE KING OF ENGLAND COULD READ IT WITHOUT HIS SPECTACLES.

Adopted on June 14, 1777, the first flag of the United States of America had 13 stripes and 13 stars representing the 13 colonies.

Our flag today has 50 stars representing our 50 states and 13 stripes reminding us of the first 13 colonies.

Some vexillologists, or flag experts, believe the first flag was created by Francis Hopkinson.

A huge flag, 30 by 42 feet, was sewn by Mary Pickersgill. It flew over Fort McHenry during the War of 1812 when the British attacked Baltimore.

Francis Scott Key wrote the words to our national anthem, "The Star-Spangled Banner," when he saw this flag still waving after the attack.

How to fold a flag

Step 1

**EQUALITY TIME LINE:** 1791 **BILL OF RIGHTS.** Guarantees basic rights of citizens. 1865 **AMENDMENT XIII TO U.S. CONSTITUTION.**

1990 **AMERICANS WITH DISABILITIES ACT.** Prohibits discrimination against people with disabilities.

of African Americans.

1965 **VOTING RIGHTS ACT.** Strikes down restrictions used to deny the voting rights

discrimination on basis of "race, color, religion, sex, or national origin."

## E is for Equality.

The Declaration of Independence established the principle that all are created equal and have God-given rights to live, to be free, and to pursue happiness. Over the years, more and more of us have been able to enjoy these rights equally.

Elliston Elementary School

OFFICE

Francis Bellamy is credited with writing the Pledge of Allegiance in Boston, 1892.

When the flag passes by in a parade, all persons should salute.

"The Stars and Stripes Forever," our national march, was first performed in 1897.

Abolishes slavery. **1920 AMENDMENT XIX.** Grants women the right to vote. **1924 INDIAN CITIZENSHIP ACT.** Declares Native Americans to be citizens.

# F is for Freedom and the Flag that we fly.

*"I pledge allegiance to the flag of the United States of America and to the Republic for which it stands, one nation under God, indivisible, with liberty and justice for all."*

**1934 INDIAN REORGANIZATION ACT.** Protects land holdings of Native American reservations. **1948 EXECUTIVE ORDER 9981.** Ends segregation in U.S. military.

**1954 BROWN V. BOARD OF EDUCATION.** Makes school segregation unconstitutional. **1964 CIVIL RIGHTS ACT.** Prohibits

Flag flown upside down indicates distress or S.O.S.

Flag flown at half-staff indicates mourning.

Flag should be carried properly folded.

Step 2

Step 3

Step 4

# G is for *God* in whom we trust.

Freedom to worship as they chose brought people to America. Freedom to worship as we choose sustains our country today.

IN 1620 THE PILGRIMS SAILED TO AMERICA IN SEARCH OF FREEDOM TO WORSHIP GOD IN THEIR OWN WAY. AFTER THEY HAD CROSSED THE VAST AND STORMY OCEAN, THEY DREW UP A PLAN FOR GOVERNING THEMSELVES CALLED THE MAYFLOWER COMPACT.

THE PILGRIMS' FIRST WINTER WAS VERY HARD, BUT IN THE SPRING, NATIVE AMERICANS OF THE WAMPANOAG TRIBE TAUGHT THEM HOW TO GROW CORN AND CATCH FISH. AFTER A SUCCESSFUL HARVEST, THE PILGRIMS INVITED THE WAMPANOAG TO JOIN IN A FEAST. TODAY WE THINK OF THEIR CELEBRATION AS THE FIRST THANKSGIVING.

GOD BLESS AMERICA

Main Street, U.S.A.

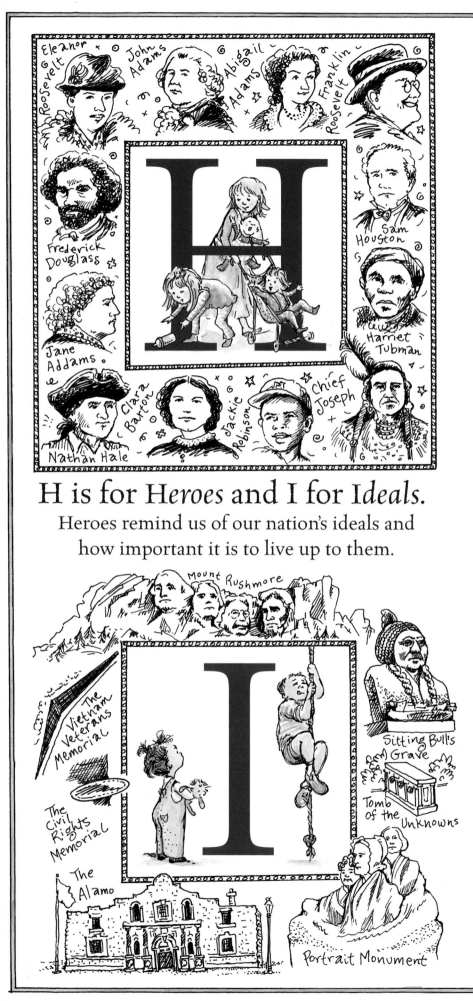

# H is for Heroes and I for Ideals.

Heroes remind us of our nation's ideals and how important it is to live up to them.

PIONEERS

FIREFIGHTERS

U.S. MILITARY

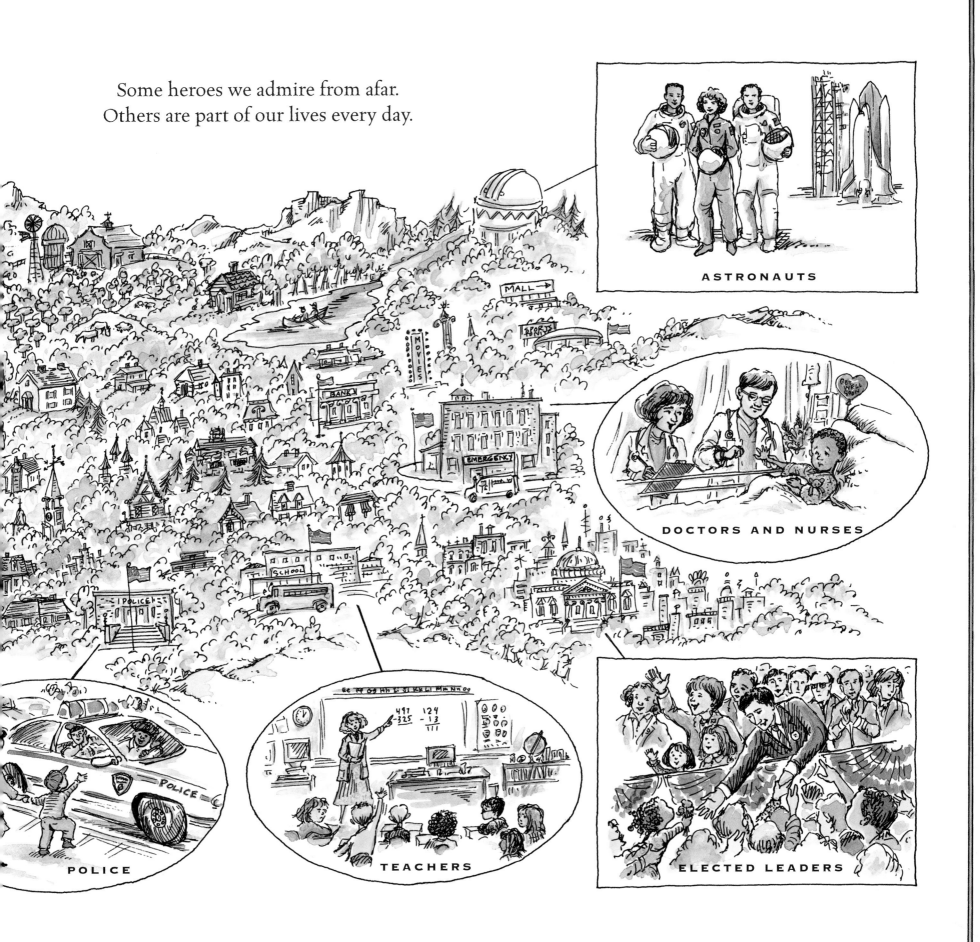

Some heroes we admire from afar.
Others are part of our lives every day.

ASTRONAUTS

DOCTORS AND NURSES

POLICE

TEACHERS

ELECTED LEADERS

THE VIRGINIA STATUTE FOR RELIGIOUS FREEDOM, WRITTEN BY JEFFERSON, WAS A FORERUNNER OF THE FIRST AMENDMENT.

WITH THE LOUISIANA PURCHASE, PRESIDENT JEFFERSON DOUBLED THE SIZE OF THE UNITED STATES. IT WAS A BARGAIN AT LESS THAN THREE CENTS AN ACRE.

Louisiana Purchase 1803 existing states New Spain

THE UNIVERSITY OF VIRGINIA, DESIGNED BY JEFFERSON, WAS ONE OF HIS PROUDEST ACCOMPLISHMENTS.

JEFFERSON'S HOME WAS MONTICELLO, WHICH HE DESIGNED AND LIVED IN MOST OF HIS LIFE.

"I cannot live without books."

## J is for *Jefferson*.

In 1776 Thomas Jefferson wrote the Declaration of Independence. He was the first secretary of state, the second vice president, and our third president.

JEFFERSON INVENTED MANY THINGS, INCLUDING A PLOW AND THIS COPYING MACHINE.

We hold these truths to be self-evident, that all men are created equal...

♪♪ Oh, deep in my heart, I do believe we shall overcome someday. ♪♪

THOUSANDS OF PEOPLE LED BY DR. KING MARCHED FROM SELMA TO MONTGOMERY, ALABAMA, IN MARCH 1965. THEY HELPED CONVINCE CONGRESS TO PASS A LAW ENSURING THAT AFRICAN AMERICANS COULD VOTE.

# K is for King.

Dr. Martin Luther King Jr. fought for justice with prayers, peaceful marches, and some of the most powerful words our nation has ever heard.

*"I have a dream that my four children will one day live in a nation where they will not be judged by the color of their skin but by the content of their character."*

"Let justice roll down like waters."

AFTER BEING JAILED FOR A PEACEFUL PROTEST, DR. KING WROTE "LETTER FROM BIRMINGHAM JAIL," IN WHICH HE DECLARED, "INJUSTICE ANYWHERE IS A THREAT TO JUSTICE EVERYWHERE."

BECAUSE HE FOUGHT VIOLENCE WITH PEACEFUL PROTEST, DR. KING WAS AWARDED THE NOBEL PEACE PRIZE. HE WAS ONLY THIRTY-FIVE YEARS OLD.

LINCOLN, BORN IN A LOG CABIN, GREW UP TO BE KNOWN AS HONEST ABE.

WHEN LINCOLN WAS ELECTED PRESIDENT, SOUTHERN STATES LEFT THE UNION, AND THE CIVIL WAR BROKE OUT.

IN 1863 LINCOLN ISSUED THE EMANCIPATION PROCLAMATION FREEING ENSLAVED AFRICAN AMERICANS IN THE CONFEDERACY.

LINCOLN'S CHILDREN TAD AND WILLIE WERE THE FIRST PRESIDENTIAL CHILDREN TO LIVE IN THE WHITE HOUSE.

"I happen temporarily to occupy this big White House. I am a living witness that any one of your children may look to come here as my father's child has."

## L is for Lincoln.

Abraham Lincoln, our sixteenth president, guided our nation during the Civil War. He was determined that we would continue to be a single nation.

THE UNION WON THE WAR, BUT ON APRIL 14, 1865, LINCOLN WAS KILLED. A FUNERAL TRAIN TOOK HIM HOME TO ILLINOIS. AMERICANS WILL REMEMBER HIM ALWAYS AS A GREAT MAN AND A GREAT PRESIDENT.

JAMES MADISON'S WIFE, DOLLEY, WAS GRACIOUS AND BRAVE. DURING THE WAR OF 1812, SHE GATHERED UP IMPORTANT DOCUMENTS AND A PAINTING OF GEORGE WASHINGTON BEFORE SHE FLED THE ADVANCING BRITISH, WHO SET FIRE TO THE WHITE HOUSE.

*"The advice nearest to my heart . . . is that the union of the states be cherished and perpetuated."*

MADISON STUDIED GOVERNMENTS OF OTHER TIMES AND PLACES TO GET IDEAS ABOUT HOW OUR OWN SHOULD BE FORMED.

## M is for *Madison*.

James Madison, our fourth president, was so important when our nation was getting started that he is called the Father of the Constitution. He was primarily responsible for the Bill of Rights.

MADISON WAS ONE OF THE AUTHORS OF THE FEDERALIST PAPERS, ESSAYS THAT HELPED CONVINCE THE STATES TO ACCEPT THE CONSTITUTION.

IN THE STREETS OUTSIDE INDEPENDENCE HALL, PHILADELPHIANS WAITED IN THE SUMMER OF 1787 TO SEE WHAT KIND OF GOVERNMENT MADISON AND THE OTHER DELEGATES HAD DECIDED ON. "WHAT HAVE WE GOT?" A WOMAN ASKED BEN FRANKLIN. "A REPUBLIC," HE REPLIED, "IF YOU CAN KEEP IT."

We the People...

Amendments

The U.S. Constitution

The U.S. Bill of Rights

POMO · HAVASUPAI · PUEBLO · MOHAWK · ABENAKI · SIOUX · CHOCTAW · ALGONQUIN · ONONDAGA · IROQUOIS · APACHE · BLACKFOOT · MENOMINEE

POCAHONTAS, DAUGHTER OF POWHATAN, HELPED THE COLONISTS AT JAMESTOWN.

SEQUOYAH, A CHEROKEE, CREATED AN ALPHABET FOR HIS PEOPLE.

TECUMSEH, A SHAWNEE LEADER, WITH HIS BROTHER, THE PROPHET, ORGANIZED NATIVE AMERICAN NATIONS INTO A CONFEDERATION.

JIM THORPE, OF SAC AND FOX HERITAGE, WAS ONE OF THE GREATEST ATHLETES OF THE TWENTIETH CENTURY.

N is for Native Americans, who came here first.

SACAJAWEA, A SHOSHONE WOMAN, GUIDED AND TRANSLATED FOR LEWIS AND CLARK AS THEY EXPLORED THE WEST.

NAVAJO CODE TALKERS, WORLD WAR II MARINES, USED THEIR NATIVE LANGUAGE TO SEND CODED MESSAGES. THE JAPANESE NEVER DECIPHERED THEIR TRANSMISSIONS.

MARIA TALLCHIEF OF THE OSAGE TRIBE BECAME A PRIMA BALLERINA.

BEN NIGHTHORSE CAMPBELL, ONE OF FORTY-FOUR CHIEFS OF THE NORTHERN CHEYENNE TRIBE, IS A U.S. SENATOR FROM COLORADO.

ARIKARA · TLINGIT · CHINOOK · TUSCARORA · PENOBSCOT · CROW · TILLAMOOK · WICHITA · POTAWATOMI · CHUMASH · ONEIDA · SENECA · UTE

HOPI · KICKAPOO · HOOPA · NEZ PERCE · OMAHA · YAKIMA · YUCHI · OJIBWA · PAIUTE · SEMINOLE · ARAPAHO · NARRAGANSETT · IOWA

MAIDU · WINNEBAGO · PIMA · CATAWBA · CREEK · PAWNEE · CADDO · COMANCHE · YOKUTS · PEQUOT · MICMAC

ACCORDING TO ONE ESTIMATE, MORE THAN 40 PERCENT OF AMERICANS LIVING TODAY HAVE AN ANCESTOR WHO PASSED THROUGH ELLIS ISLAND, THE ENTRY POINT TO AMERICA FOR MILLIONS OF IMMIGRANTS.

*"I hereby declare, on oath, . . . that I will support and defend the Constitution and laws of the United States of America."*
*—from the Oath of Citizenship*

O is for the *Oath* new Americans take.

"Our obligations to our country never cease but with our lives." John Adams

Lemonade
25¢
for Red Cross

P is for the Patriotism
that fills our hearts
with pride.

Louis Armstrong: jazz trumpeter, singer, and band-leader

Emily Dickinson: groundbreaking poet

Babe Ruth: baseball legend

Althea Gibson: tennis champion

Orville and Wilbur Wright: first successful powered flight

Benjamin Franklin: inventor, scientist, statesman

Q is for America's Quest for the new, the far, and the very best.

Martha Graham: modern-dance innovator

I. M. Pei: world-renowned architect

Thomas Edison: inventor of the light-bulb, motion-picture projector, and phonograph

*"We choose to go to the moon . . . and do the other things, not because they are easy, but because they are hard, because that goal will serve to organize and measure the best of our energies and skills."*—John F. Kennedy

**FREEDOM OF SPEECH**

**FREEDOM OF THE PRESS**

**FREEDOM OF RELIGION**

**FREEDOM OF ASSEMBLY**

R is for the *Rights* we are guaranteed.

Our basic rights are set forth in the Constitution and its amendments. The first ten amendments are called the Bill of Rights.

**RIGHT TO KEEP AND BEAR ARMS**

**RIGHT TO TRIAL BY JURY**

**RIGHT TO VOTE**

LUCRETIA MOTT

LUCY STONE

ALICE PAUL

SUSAN B. ANTHONY

"We hold these truths to be self-evident: that all men and women are created equal..."
—Declaration of Sentiments Seneca Falls July 1848

# S is for *Suffrage*.

In 1848 in Seneca Falls, New York, women began the long struggle for suffrage, or the right to vote. In 1920 their voting rights were recognized all across the nation.

ELIZABETH CADY STANTON

SOJOURNER TRUTH

CARRIE CHAPMAN CATT

AMELIA BLOOMER

ESTHER HOBART MORRIS

## T is for Tolerance.

Free to think and believe and pursue happiness in our own way, we recognize the right of others to do the same.

## U is for United States.

Our country is big. Our people come from every part of the world. But, different as we are, we are all part of a single nation: the United States of America.

Trung Thu
Vietnamese lunar festival in the fall

Children wear masks.

Moon cakes

Martin Luther King Jr. Day
3rd Monday of January

Pulaski Day
October 11

Labor Day
1st Monday in September

Mormon Pioneer Day
Ju 2

September 19
Parades for the Feast of San Gennaro

St. Valentine's Day
Welsh love spoon
Feb.14

Hanukkah
8 days in December
menorah
dreidel

Mardi Gras
the Tuesday before Lent

Veterans Day
Nov. 11

Easter falls on the first Sunday after the first full moon after the spring equinox.

A candle is lighted on each of the 7 days of Kwanzaa.
Dec. 26–Jan. 1

Presidents' Day
3rd Monday in February, honoring all U.S. Presidents

March 17
St. Patrick's Day

Polar Bears
Juneau
Alaska

World Kite Museum and Hall of Fame
Seattle's Space Needle
Mt. St. Helens
WASHINGTON

Glacier National Park
grizzly Bears
MONTAN

lumber
Hells Canyon deepest in USA
Potatoes

Custer Battlefie

OREGON
Crater Lake deepest in USA

IDAHO
Sun Valley
Skiing
Balanced Rock

Old Faithful geyser
Yellowstone National Park
WYOMIN

CALIFORNIA
NEVADA
Ghost Towns
Lake Tahoe

Great Salt Lake

Grea Divid Basi

San Francisco's Golden Gate Bridge
Yosemite
National Parks
Sequoia

Shows
8
Las Vegas

UTAH
rock formations
The Needles at Canyonland and Rainbow Bridge National Monument
Gran Canyon

COLORA
An Cli Dwelli

balloon

Death Valley
Hoover Dam
Colorado River

HOLLYWOOD

Kauai Oahu
Maui
Hawaii

missions

ARIZONA
Cacti
Sonoran Desert

Kitt Peak National Observatory
Tombstone
Skeleton Canyon

NEW MEXICO

Mexico

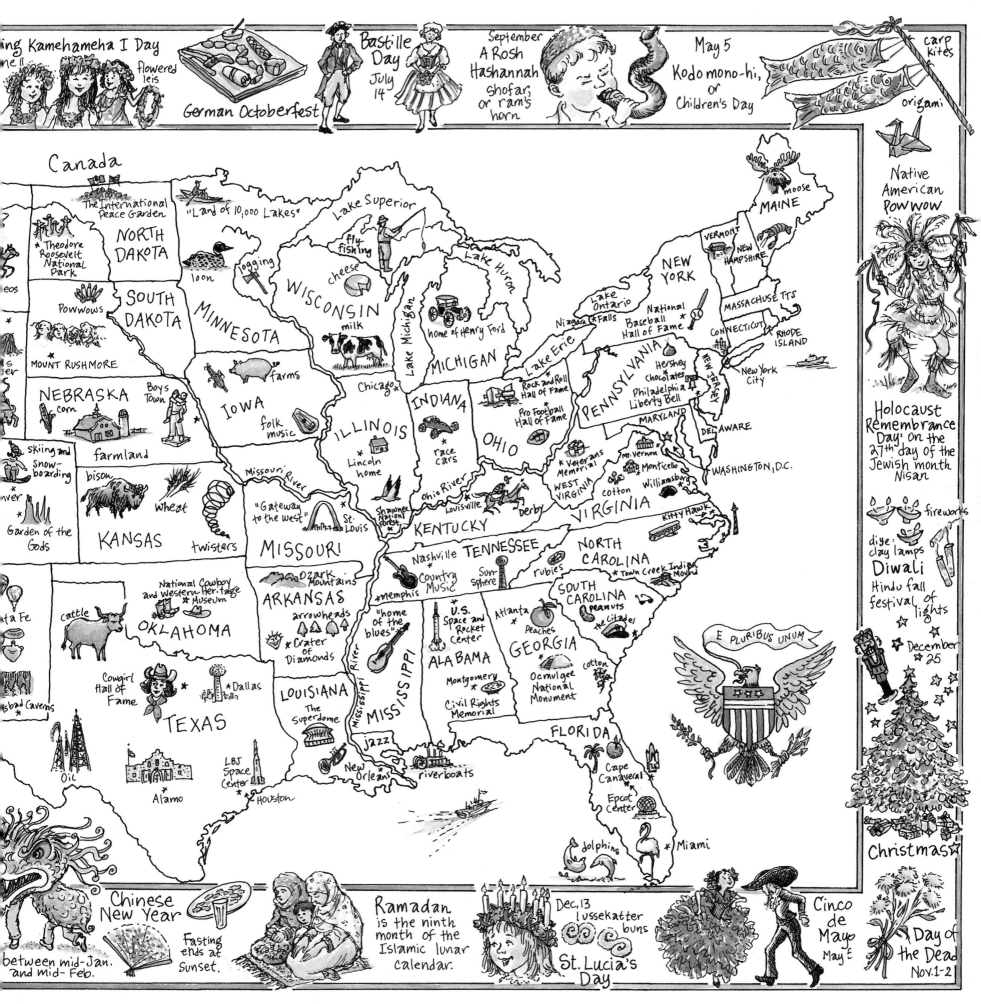

Navy Cross

Silver Star

MOLLY PITCHER: ONE OF THE FIRST AMERICAN WOMEN TO FIGHT FOR FREEDOM.

COURAGEOUS WORLD WAR II MARINES HELPED WIN THE WAR IN THE PACIFIC.

V is for the *Valor* shown by those who've kept us free.

IN WORLD WAR II, BRAVE PARATROOPERS PARACHUTED BEHIND ENEMY LINES.

54TH MASSACHUSETTS REGIMENT: AN AFRICAN-AMERICAN UNIT THAT FOUGHT WITH GREAT VALOR IN THE CIVIL WAR.

442ND REGIMENTAL COMBAT TEAM: A JAPANESE-AMERICAN UNIT THAT BECAME ONE OF THE MOST DECORATED IN MILITARY HISTORY.

AMERICAN SAILORS WON THE BATTLE OF MIDWAY AND TURNED THE COURSE OF WORLD WAR II.

ALVIN C. YORK: WORLD WAR I

Medal of Honor

AUDIE MURPHY: WORLD WAR II

BRAVE AMERICAN SOLDIERS FOUGHT IN THE JUNGLES OF VIETNAM.

A TALL, DIGNIFIED MAN, GENERAL GEORGE WASHINGTON LED THE REVOLUTIONARY FORCES THAT DEFEATED A MUCH STRONGER FOE.

HE PRESIDED OVER THE CONSTITUTIONAL CONVENTION, BRINGING THE GREAT ESTEEM HIS FELLOW CITIZENS HAD FOR HIM TO THE EFFORT TO CREATE A WORKABLE GOVERNMENT.

UNANIMOUSLY ELECTED PRESIDENT, WASHINGTON TOOK THE OATH OF OFFICE IN 1789 IN NEW YORK CITY, THE NATION'S TEMPORARY CAPITAL.

"First in war, first in peace, and first in the hearts of his countrymen."

~Henry Lee

"I walk on untrodden ground."

## W is for Washington.

George Washington, our first president, is called the father of our country. Brave in battle and dignified always, he was celebrated as "the man who unites all hearts."

WASHINGTON LOVED HIS HOME AT MOUNT VERNON, VIRGINIA, BUT LEFT IT WHEN HIS COUNTRY NEEDED HIM. IN 1797, AFTER HE HAD BEEN PRESIDENT FOR TWO TERMS, HE RETURNED HOME TO STAY.

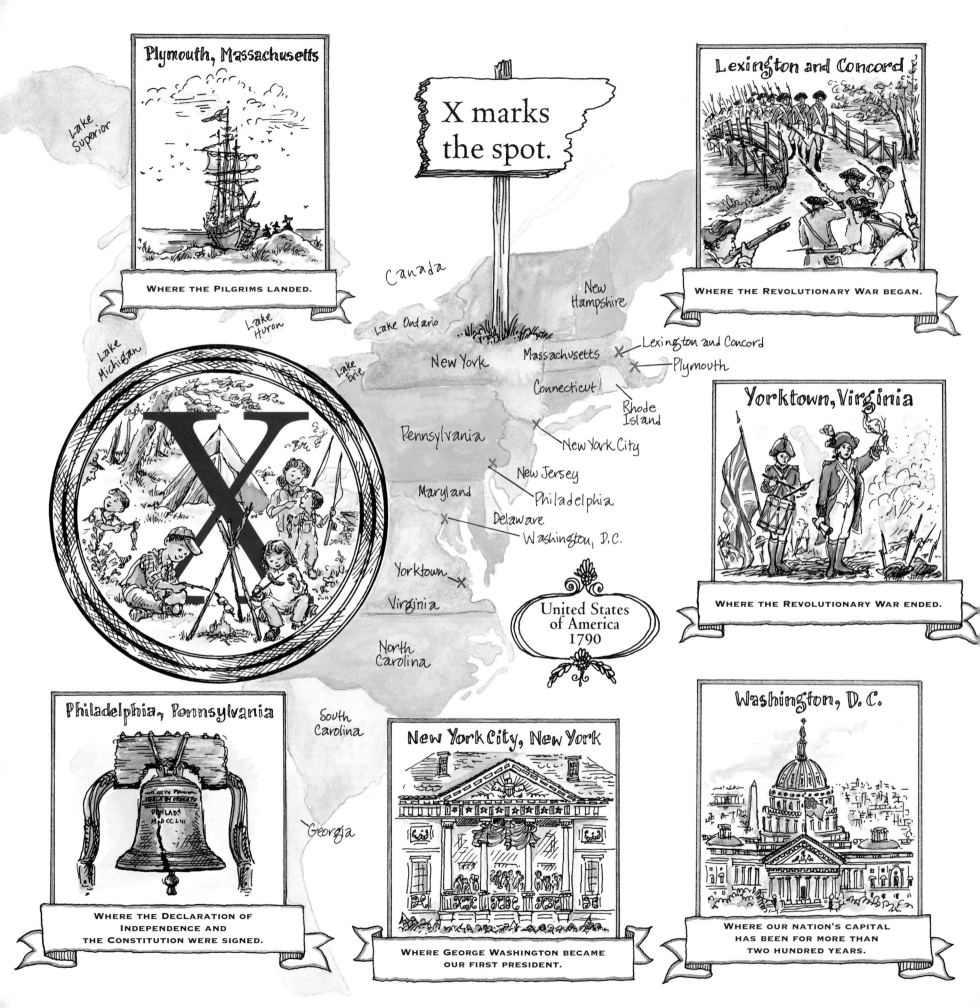

**Plymouth, Massachusetts**

WHERE THE PILGRIMS LANDED.

X marks the spot.

**Lexington and Concord**

WHERE THE REVOLUTIONARY WAR BEGAN.

Lake Superior

Canada

New Hampshire

Lake Huron

Lake Ontario

Lexington and Concord

Massachusetts

Plymouth

Lake Michigan

Lake Erie

New York

Connecticut

Rhode Island

Pennsylvania

New York City

New Jersey

Philadelphia

Maryland

Delaware

Washington, D.C.

**Yorktown, Virginia**

WHERE THE REVOLUTIONARY WAR ENDED.

Yorktown

Virginia

United States of America 1790

North Carolina

**Philadelphia, Pennsylvania**

South Carolina

Georgia

WHERE THE DECLARATION OF INDEPENDENCE AND THE CONSTITUTION WERE SIGNED.

**New York City, New York**

WHERE GEORGE WASHINGTON BECAME OUR FIRST PRESIDENT.

**Washington, D.C.**

WHERE OUR NATION'S CAPITAL HAS BEEN FOR MORE THAN TWO HUNDRED YEARS.

Y is for *You* and all you will be in this greatest of countries, the land of the free.

*"The noblest question in the world is: What good may I do in it?"*

—Benjamin Franklin

Z is the end of the alphabet, but not of America's story. Strong and free, we will continue to be an inspiration to the world.

*"I know that for America there will always be a bright dawn ahead."*–Ronald Reagan

America! America! God shed his grace on thee and crown thy good with brotherhood from sea to shining sea!

## Notes on the Text

*I wrote this book so that children could enjoy it by themselves, but I like to think that it will most often be read and discussed by parents and children together. Those who wish to continue the discussion beyond the page devoted to each letter of the alphabet should find the following explanatory material of use.*—L. C.

**A**

A portion of Emma Lazarus's 1883 poem "The New Colossus" is inscribed on the Statue of Liberty: "Give me your tired, your poor, / Your huddled masses yearning to breathe free, / The wretched refuse of your teeming shore. / Send these, the homeless, tempest-tossed to me: / I lift my lamp beside the golden door!"

Katharine Lee Bates, who taught at Wellesley College, wrote "America the Beautiful" in 1893. The beginning of the last stanza is quoted in the banner at the bottom of the page.

**B**

John Adams, who wrote about "pomp and parade" on July 3, 1776, thought that America's birthday would be celebrated on July 2, the day the Continental Congress voted that the colonies were free and independent states. But Americans have long celebrated instead on July 4, the day the Congress formally approved the Declaration of Independence.

**C**

Signed in Philadelphia on September 17, 1787, the Constitution had to be ratified, or accepted, by nine of the thirteen original states. That threshold was met in June 1788, when New Hampshire became the ninth state to ratify. Now the oldest enduring written national constitution, the U.S. Constitution has served as a model for others around the world.

James Madison wrote about the "miracle" of the Constitution in 1829.

The Declaration of Independence, the Constitution, and the Bill of Rights, usually on public display at the National Archives, will be available for public viewing again in 2003 when renovation of the rotunda and exhibit halls is completed.

The Constitution provides for three branches of government: the executive (symbolized by the White House, where the president lives and works), the legislative (by the Capitol, where Congress meets), and the judicial (by the Supreme Court Building, where the nine justices meet and deliberate).

**D**

The Tom Paine quotation is from *Common Sense,* a pamphlet published in January 1776 that helped convince Americans it was time to seek independence from England.

John Adams wrote about the difficulties that would follow the American colonists' decision to seek independence in a letter to his wife, Abigail, on July 3, 1776.

On July 4, John Hancock, as president of the Congress, signed the Declaration, and Charles Thomson, secretary of the Congress, certi-

fied it. The document was then transferred to parchment, and eventually fifty-six delegates signed, pledging lives, fortunes, and "sacred honor" to the cause of independence.

**E and F**

Even after the Indian Citizenship Act, some states did not allow Native Americans to vote. It took until 1962, but finally all fifty states recognized Native American voting rights.

When the flag passes in review, persons in uniform render the military salute. Those not in uniform stand at attention and place the right hand over the heart. The same etiquette applies during the pledge of allegiance and the playing of the national anthem.

Mary Pickersgill was assisted in making the flag for Fort McHenry by her thirteen-year-old daughter, Caroline. Mrs. Pickersgill was paid $405.90 for making the flag.

John Philip Sousa composed "The Stars and Stripes Forever."

**G**

The Mayflower Compact, a landmark document in the history of self-government, was named after the Pilgrims' small ship, the *Mayflower.*

Squanto, or Tisquantum, who spoke English, was the Native American who helped the Pilgrims the most. He had been kidnapped, sold into slavery in Spain, and had escaped to England. He had made his way back to America not long before the Pilgrims arrived. They called him "a special instrument sent of God."

**H and I**

Eleanor Roosevelt (1884–1962): Wife of President Franklin D. Roosevelt, she worked to help the less fortunate and to advance the cause of women.

John Adams (1735–1826): A prime mover in the drive for American independence, Adams became the first vice president of the United States and its second president.

Abigail Adams (1744–1818): Wife of John Adams, she was a woman of great strength and wisdom. John and Abigail's son, John Quincy Adams, became the sixth president of the United States.

Franklin D. Roosevelt (1882–1945): America's thirty-second president, he was a resolute leader during two of the nation's darkest times, the Great Depression and World War II.

Sam Houston (1793–1863): He led the Texas army in the successful fight for independence from Mexico, served as president of the independent Republic of Texas, and, after Texas was admitted to the Union, as a senator and governor. When he stood firm against the wish of Texas voters to leave the Union, he was deposed from office.

Harriet Tubman (1820?–1913): She escaped slavery by fleeing to the North and then repeatedly risked her freedom and her life by returning to the South to help hundreds of others escape.

Chief Joseph (1840?–1904): After fighting broke out between the Nez Perce and the U.S. Army, this brave chief led his people on a 1,400-mile march with the goal of finding refuge in Canada. Forced to surrender before he reached the border, he said, "My heart is sick and sad. From where the sun now stands, I will fight no more forever."

Jackie Robinson (1919–1972): In 1947 he became the first African-American to play modern-day major league baseball. Enduring insult and abuse, he helped his Brooklyn Dodger teammates win the National League pennant and was named rookie of the year. In 1962 he was inducted into the National Baseball Hall of Fame.

Clara Barton (1821–1912): After working as a volunteer distributing supplies and aid to wounded soldiers during the Civil War, this humanitarian (known as the "Angel of the Battlefield") founded the American Red Cross and served as its first president.

Nathan Hale (1755–1776): Captured by the British during the Revolutionary War, Hale, a Connecticut officer, was sentenced to death. He is reported to have said, "I only regret that I have but one life to lose for my country."

Jane Addams (1860–1935): A pioneer social worker, she dedicated her life to the poor. When she founded Hull House, a place where poor people in Chicago could find help, she began a nationwide movement to improve the lives of the less fortunate.

Frederick Douglass (1817–1895): Born in slavery, Douglass taught himself how to write and speak persuasively. After escaping to the North, he used his powerful intellect and noted oratorical skills to seek justice for African-Americans. His autobiography, *Narrative of the Life of Frederick Douglass,* is a literary classic.

Mount Rushmore is located in the Black Hills of South Dakota. Designed by Gutzon Borglum and completed in 1941, it presents heroic sculptures of George Washington, Thomas Jefferson, Theodore Roosevelt, and Abraham Lincoln. Roosevelt, a dedicated outdoorsman, was our twenty-sixth president and a passionate advocate of preserving our nation's natural resources.

Sitting Bull (1831?–1890): A powerful religious and political leader, Sitting Bull, a Sioux chief, organized the Indians who defeated George Armstrong Custer at the Battle of the Little Bighorn in 1876. His grave and memorial, near Mobridge, South Dakota, overlook the Missouri River.

The Tomb of the Unknowns at Arlington National Cemetery in Arlington, Virginia, commemorates the unidentified dead of four wars. The inscription reads: "Here rests in honored glory an American soldier known but to God."

The Portrait Monument to Lucretia Mott, Elizabeth Cady Stanton, and Susan B. Anthony, three leaders of the woman suffrage movement, is in the rotunda of the U.S. Capitol. It was sculpted by Adelaide Johnson in 1920.

The Alamo, located in San Antonio, Texas, is the site of a crucial battle in Texas's war for independence from Mexico. Although overwhelmingly outnumbered by General Santa Anna's army, the defenders of the Alamo held out for thirteen days in 1836. Their brave stand led to the battle cry, "Remember the Alamo!"

The Civil Rights Memorial in Montgomery, Alabama, provides a time line of events and honors those who gave their lives during the civil rights movement. It was dedicated in 1989.

The Vietnam Veterans Memorial commemorates the more than 58,000 Americans who died in the Vietnam War. Of all the memorials in Washington, D.C., this is the one most often visited.

## J

In 1774 Jefferson wrote about God's gifts of life and liberty; in 1776 he wrote the Declaration of Independence; in 1787 he encouraged his daughter Martha "never to be idle."

Elected in 1800, Jefferson was the first president to be inaugurated in the nation's new capital, Washington, D.C. Jefferson served until 1809.

In 1811 he wrote about the last hope of human liberty in a letter to newspaper editor William Duane; in 1815 he told John Adams that he could not "live without books."

Jefferson was eighty-three when he died on July 4, 1826. John Adams also died on that day. He was ninety years old. Said Daniel Webster of the two men, "Their work doth not perish with them."

The Virginia Statute for Religious Freedom, which became law in 1786, provided for the separation of church and state.

The Louisiana Purchase, out of which thirteen states and parts of states would be formed, occurred in 1803, when the United States purchased the land from France.

The University of Virginia was founded in 1819. A select number of students today have the honor of living in "Lawn rooms" that Jefferson designed.

Thomas Jefferson loved mockingbirds. Two of them are holding the garland above the letter J.

## K

Dr. King was born in Atlanta, Georgia, in 1929. He wrote "Letter from Birmingham Jail" in 1963, the same year he delivered his famed "I have a dream" speech in Washington, D.C. He won the Nobel Peace Prize in 1964.

A minister with a Ph.D. in theology, Dr. King frequently quoted scripture. "Let justice roll down like waters," which he quoted in "Letter from Birmingham Jail," is from the Old Testament book of Amos 5:24.

Dr. King was thirty-nine years old when he was assassinated in Memphis, Tennessee, in 1968.

## L

Lincoln was born in 1809 in a log cabin in Kentucky. He moved to Illinois as a young man.

Lincoln made his remarks about children to the 166th Ohio Regiment in 1864.

Lincoln had four sons. The first, Edward, died in 1850. Robert was a university student when his father was elected so only Tad and Willie lived in the White House. Willie died while his father was president.

Lincoln was elected president in 1860. The Civil War began in 1861 and ended in 1865. Lincoln was assassinated at Ford's Theater in Washington, D.C., on April 14, 1865, less than a week after General Robert E. Lee surrendered at Appomattox Court House in Virginia.

## M

Madison was born in Virginia in 1751.

His most intensive study of other governments occurred before the Constitutional Convention (1787), when he read dozens upon dozens of books that Thomas Jefferson, at Madison's request, sent from Paris, where Jefferson was representing the United States.

The other authors of the Federalist Papers were Alexander Hamilton and John Jay.

Madison was president from 1809 to 1817. He wrote about "liberty and learning" in 1822.

"The advice nearest my heart" quotation is from a note opened after Madison's death in 1836.

The exchange between the Philadelphia woman and Benjamin Franklin was recorded by Maryland delegate James McHenry.

## N

Early migrants to North America began to come across the Bering land bridge from Asia at least 15,000 years ago. In recent years, some investigators have suggested much earlier arrivals, perhaps even by boat.

The tribes named in the border of this page symbolize the diversity of Native American life. There are hundreds of native groups in North America with different customs and cultural heritages.

## O

The full text of the Oath of Allegiance, also known as the Oath of Citizenship: "I hearby declare, on oath, that I absolutely and entirely renounce and abjure all allegiance and fidelity to any foreign prince, potentate, state, or sovereignty of whom or which I have heretofore been a subject or citizen; that I will support and defend the Constitution and laws of the United States of America against all enemies, foreign and domestic; that I will bear true faith and allegiance to the same; that I will bear arms on behalf of the United States when required by the law; that I will perform noncombatant service in the Armed Forces of the United States when required by the law; that I will perform work of national importance under civilian direction when required by the law; and that I take this obligation freely without any mental reservation or purpose of evasion; so help me God."

## P

John Adams wrote about our obligations to our country in a letter to physician Benjamin Rush in 1808.

## Q

The names in the border symbolize thousands upon thousands of Americans whose achievements reflect excellence. Children should be encouraged to add to this list.

Jonas Salk (1914–1995): A physician and scientist, he developed the first polio vaccine.

Babe Didrikson Zaharias (1913–1956): An Olympic track-and-field athlete and champion golfer, she was one of the finest woman athletes of the twentieth century.

Orson Welles (1915–1985): An innovative filmmaker and actor, he directed and starred in *Citizen Kane,* a 1941 film that changed cinematic history.

Walt Whitman (1819–1892): A poet who broke with tradition, Whitman wrote *Leaves of Grass,* which he revised throughout his life.

Frank Capra (1897–1991): Famed in the motion-picture world, Capra directed *It Happened One Night, Mr. Smith Goes to Washington,* and the Christmas classic, *It's a Wonderful Life.*

Samuel F. B. Morse (1791–1872): Best known for inventing the telegraph and Morse code, he was also an accomplished painter.

Alexander Graham Bell (1847–1922): A teacher of the deaf, Bell invented the telephone.

Albert Einstein (1879–1955): One of the greatest scientists of all time, Einstein developed the theory of relativity, which revolutionized thinking about space and time.

Roberto Clemente (1934–1972): Outfielder for the Pittsburgh Pirates and the first Latino baseball player elected to the Baseball Hall of Fame, Clemente was dedicated to helping others. He died in a plane crash as he traveled to Nicaragua to aid victims of an earthquake.

Walt Disney (1901–1966): A cartoonist, filmmaker, and entrepreneur, he founded the company that has given us much-loved characters like Mickey Mouse, Donald Duck, and Goofy. He won a record twenty-six Academy Awards.

Jackson Pollock (1912–1956): An artist who influenced many others, he created large-scale abstract paintings by pouring or spattering paint instead of using a brush.

John Glenn (1921– ): In 1962 Glenn became the first American to orbit the earth. In 1998, during his fourth and last term in the U.S. Senate, he became the oldest person to go into space.

Mark Twain (1835–1910): An author whose real name was Samuel Langhorne Clemens, Twain wrote *The Adventures of Huckleberry Finn* and "The Celebrated Jumping Frog of Calaveras County," among many other works.

George Washington Carver (1864–1943): An agricultural researcher, Carver developed hundreds of uses for peanuts. His insights about crop rotation changed the agricultural practices of Southern farmers.

Amelia Earhart (1897–1937): A pilot, she was the first woman to fly solo across the Atlantic as well as the first woman to fly solo across the Pacific. While she was attempting an around-the-world flight, her airplane disappeared. It was never found.

George Balanchine (1904–1983): One of ballet's most important choreographers, he created more than two hundred dance works.

Under his artistic leadership the New York City Ballet became one of the outstanding dance companies in the world.

Helen Keller (1880–1968): Although a childhood illness left her both blind and deaf, she became an author, lecturer, and social activist.

Yo-Yo Ma (1955– ): A world-renowned cellist, he performs as a soloist and has played with other noted American musicians, such as violinist Pinchas Zukerman and pianist Emanuel Ax.

Louise Nevelson (1900–1988): The first important woman sculptor of the twentieth century, Nevelson assembled strikingly designed vertical boxes into dramatic wall sculptures.

Mark Hopkins (1802–1887): Hopkins was a college president and teacher of legendary skill. One of his pupils, James A. Garfield, who became the twentieth president of the United States, declared that "the ideal college is Mark Hopkins on one end of a log and a student on the other."

Mary Cassatt (1844–1926): An American impressionist painter, she is particularly remembered for her perceptive portraits of women and children.

Neil Armstrong (1930– ): The first man on the moon, astronaut Armstrong left behind a plaque that reads: "Here men from the planet earth first set foot upon the moon, July 1969, A.D. We came in peace for all mankind."

John James Audubon (1785–1851): An artist and student of nature, he depicted more than a thousand birds in his work *The Birds of America.*

Luis Alvarez (1911–1988): A physicist, he was awarded a Nobel Prize in Physics in 1968 for his work in high-energy physics.

Richard Rodgers (1902–1979) and Oscar Hammerstein II (1895–1960): A composer and a lyricist, they teamed to create such outstanding musicals as *Carousel, Oklahoma!, The Sound of Music,* and *The King and* I.

Marian Anderson (1897–1993): After being denied permission to sing in Washington's Constitution Hall in 1939, Anderson thrilled a crowd that gathered to hear her at the Lincoln Memorial. In 1955 she became the first African-American to sing as a soloist as a member of New York's Metropolitan Opera Company.

Stephen Crane (1871–1900): A novelist and short-story writer, Crane authored remarkably realistic fiction. *The Red Badge of Courage* is his most famous work.

Ernest Hemingway (1899–1961): An avid sportsman, he was one of America's most famous writers. His works include *The Sun Also Rises, A Farewell to Arms,* and *The Old Man and the Sea.*

Langston Hughes (1902–1967): A writer best known for his poetry, Hughes utilized the traditions of African-American culture in his work. His books include *Weary Blues* and *The Big Sea.*

Frank Lloyd Wright (1867–1959): One of the greatest twentieth-century architects, Wright insisted that his buildings be integrated with their natural surroundings.

Ansel Adams (1902–1984): America's foremost nature photographer, Adams captured the beauty and drama of the American West in his black-and-white photographs.

Scott Joplin (1868–1917): Known as "the king of ragtime," Joplin created such pieces as "The Entertainer" and "Maple Leaf Rag."

Willa Cather (1873–1947): One of the greatest American novelists, Cather wrote of the frontier experience in works such as O *Pioneers!* and *My Ántonia.*

John F. Kennedy talked about the importance of going to the moon at Rice University on September 12, 1962.

## R

The first ten amendments to the Constitution, adopted in 1791, are known as the Bill of Rights. They are, in brief:

I. Freedom of religion, freedom of speech, freedom of the press, freedom of assembly
II. The right to bear arms
III. No soldiers billeted in private homes during peacetime
IV. No unreasonable search and seizure
V. The right not to be a witness against oneself
VI. The right to a speedy and public trial
VII. The right to trial by jury
VIII. No cruel or unusual punishment
IX. Rights set forth in Constitution not to be construed to deny others retained by the people
X. Powers not delegated to the United States by the Constitution reserved to the states or the people

The right to vote is protected by a number of amendments, including XV, XIX, XXIV, and XXVI.

## S

Lucretia Mott (1793–1880): A Quaker antislavery advocate and an early women's rights activist, she joined with Elizabeth Cady Stanton to organize the first women's rights convention. It was held in Seneca Falls, New York, in 1848.

Lucy Stone (1818–1893): An abolitionist and widely traveled lecturer on woman suffrage, Stone was one of the first women's rights advocates to keep her maiden name after marrying.

Alice Paul (1885–1977): A militant in the struggle for women's rights, she picketed the White House to highlight the suffrage cause. When women got the vote, she began a lifelong struggle for an Equal Rights Amendment to the Constitution.

Susan B. Anthony (1820–1906): She dedicated her adult years to getting women the right to vote, and although she did not see success in her lifetime, she was confident in the outcome. "Failure is impossible!" she said shortly before her death.

Elizabeth Cady Stanton (1815–1902): She drafted the "Declaration of Sentiments," which declared that "men and women are created equal," for the Seneca Falls Convention in 1848 and for fifty years led the effort to get the vote for women.

Esther Hobart Morris (1814–1902): As Justice of the Peace in South Pass, Wyoming, in 1870, she was the first woman in America to hold judicial office. Wyoming Territory granted women voting rights in 1869, and when Wyoming entered the Union in 1890, it became the first state in which women had full suffrage.

Amelia Bloomer (1818–1894): A newspaper publisher and editor, she was an advocate of dress reform. When she published a picture of the outfit some suffragists favored (long pants under a knee-length skirt), the pants became known as "bloomers."

Carrie Chapman Catt (1859–1947): A leader of the second generation of suffragists, she fought tirelessly to win the vote for women.

Sojourner Truth (1797?–1883): After escaping slavery, she joined the abolitionist movement and was a champion of the rights of African Americans and women. When it was said that women were too weak to be full citizens, she recounted the hardships she had endured and asked, "Ain't I a woman?"

## T and U
The border of these pages pays tribute to holidays that are important to different groups in this country as well as to holidays like Presidents' Day, Martin Luther King Jr. Day, Labor Day, and Veterans Day that we recognize as a nation.

*E pluribus unum* is a Latin phrase meaning "out of many, one." It appears on the Great Seal of the United States, and today symbolizes one nation encompassing people of many different races, religions, and national origins.

## V
Alvin C. York and Audie Murphy, as well as those named in the border, are some of the thousands of Americans who have been awarded the Congressional Medal of Honor since 1863, when it was first presented. Given personally by the president of the United States, the medal is the nation's highest decoration and recognizes "individual gallantry at the risk of life above and beyond the call of duty." Accounts of the valorous service of Medal of Honor recipients can be found on the Web site of the Congressional Medal of Honor Society: www.cmohs.org.

## W
Washington was born in Virginia in 1732. He led American forces from 1775 to 1783. President from 1789 to 1797, he wrote, "I walk on untrodden ground," in a January 9, 1790, letter to Catherine Macaulay Graham less than a year after assuming office.

During Washington's time, it was popular to toast him as "the man who unites all hearts."

Washington died in 1799. "First in war, first in peace, and first in the hearts of his countrymen" was part of a tribute to him composed after his death by Henry Lee, a Virginia congressman who had known Washington for many years.

## X
The clash of British troops and American minutemen at Lexington and Concord in April 1775 was an earthshaking event. Ralph Waldo Emerson commemorated it with the poem, "Concord Hymn," which begins, "By the rude bridge that arched the flood, / Their flag to April's breeze unfurled, / Here once the embattled farmers stood / And fired the shot heard round the world."

When British troops under the command of Lord Cornwallis surrendered to Americans under the command of General Washington at Yorktown on October 19, 1781, the war was effectively over. The Treaty of Paris, which formally ended the war and recognized American independence, was signed on September 3, 1783.

Congress approved the Potomac location of the nation's capital in 1790, but it was ten years before our national government was officially located there. Meanwhile the capital moved from New York, where George Washington was sworn in, to Philadelphia. In 1800 Washington, D.C., became the seat of national government.

## Y
Benjamin Franklin gave this advice in the 1737 edition of *Poor Richard's Almanac*.

## Z
The quotation from Ronald Reagan is contained in the 1994 letter he wrote to the nation saying that he had Alzheimer's disease: "I now begin the journey that will lead me into the sunset of my life. I know that for America there will always be a bright dawn ahead."

The opening pages of this book depict a celebration in New York harbor. The closing ones show a sunrise along the coast of California. The concluding words are the last lines of "America the Beautiful."

MYTHS ACROSS THE MAP

# VAMPIRE MYTHS

Jenny Mason

Gareth Stevens
PUBLISHING

Please visit our website, **www.garethstevens.com**.
For a free color catalog of all our high-quality books,
call toll free 1-800-542-2595 or fax 1-877-542-2596.

CATALOGING-IN-PUBLICATION DATA

Names: Mason, Jenny.
Title: Vampire myths / Jenny Mason.
Description: New York : Gareth Stevens Publishing, 2018. | Series: Myths across the map |
    Includes index.
Identifiers: LCCN ISBN 9781538214473 (pbk.) | ISBN 9781538213742 (library bound) |
    ISBN 9781538214480 (6 pack)
Subjects: LCSH: Vampires--Juvenile literature.
Classification: LCC GR830.V3 M37 2018 | DDC 398.21--dc23

Published in 2018 by
**Gareth Stevens Publishing**
111 East 14th Street, Suite 349
New York, NY 10003

Developed and Produced by Focus Strategic Communications, Inc.
Project Manager: Adrianna Edwards
Editor: Ron Edwards
Design and Composition: Ruth Dwight
Copyeditors: Adrianna Edwards, Francine Geraci
Media Researchers: Adrianna Edwards, Paula Joiner, Maddi Nixon
Proofreader: Francine Geraci
Index: Ron Edwards, Maddi Nixon

PHOTO CREDITS: Credit Abbreviations: S Shutterstock; WC Wikimedia Commons. Position on
the page: T: top, B: bottom, C: center, L: left, R: right. Cover, Title Page: S; 4: Denis Simonov/S;
5: Joe Seer/S; 6: Ammit Jack/S; 7: dreamerb/S; 8: Nataliya Kuznetsova/S; 9: Joe Seer/S; 10:
Svetlana Rib/S; 11: Morphart Creation/S; 12: Kateryna Kon/S; 13: Fer Gregory/S; 14: Blue Sky
Studio/S; 15: Vera Petruk/S; 16: Skeat, Walter William and Blagden, Charles Otto, ed. Malay
Magic, Being an Introduction to the Folklore and Popular Religion of the Malay Peninsula.
London: Macmillan. 1900. 326. Internet Archive. Web. 16 May 2017; 17: Anton V. Tokarev/S; 18:
Marcin Sylwia Ciesielski/S; 19 CL: Alexlky/S, BR: vectorfreak/S; 20: Alexander Mazurkevich/S;
21: Ethan Daniels/S; 22: Ari N/S; 23: Taras Stelmah/S; 24: belizar/S; 25: Jef Thompson/S; 26:
meaofoto/S; 27: Peyker/S; 28: Yellowj/S; 29: Eugen Hollander Engraving/WC; 30: MasterQ/S;
31, 32: Everett Historical/S; 33: Bergpavian/WC; 34: Richcat/S; 35: Photosebia/S; 36: Madboy74/
WC; 37: Fotokon/S; 38: Constantine Pankin/S; 39: Olga Popova/S; 40: Figalip/S; 41: Everett
Collection/S; 42: Jaguar PS/S; 43: Florida Department of Corrections; 44: Kiselev Andrey
Valerevich/S; 45: vectorEps/S; Design Elements: Margarita Miller/S, viewgene/S, yoshi0511/S.

Printed in the United States of America

CPSIA compliance information: Batch CW18GS: For further information contact
Gareth Stevens, New York, New York at 1-800-542-2595.

# TABLE OF CONTENTS

# WHAT IS A VAMPIRE?

## DEADLY ENCOUNTERS

Whether you've seen them in movies, read about them in books, battled them in video games, or faced them in your nightmares, vampires are among the most recognizable monsters in the world.

Today, we know them by their fangs and lust to drink human blood. They rise from the grave and stalk the night world. We believe their skin is ageless and pale—the unfortunate combination of being immortal and unable to ever step into the sunlight without bursting into flames. They used to wear capes and live in gloomy castles, but now they look and dress like us. Sometimes, they are merciless killers. Other times, they are misunderstood rebels or antiheroes.

Whatever they are or however they have been perceived, vampires are mythical.

# MYTHTAKEN IDENTITY

Myths are commonly held beliefs rooted deep in the past. They are the stories we tell ourselves to explain the inexplicable. Myths may have all the trappings of truth, including long lists of evidence and eyewitnesses. But when it comes to expanding our understanding of the world's greater mysteries, myths sometimes shed as much light as a new moon.

The myth of the vampire runs deep in our veins. It arose out of our longing to understand illness and death and their mystical relationship to the blood streaming through our bodies. As our understanding progressed, so too did the vampire mythology. As we learned to defy illness and nearly outwit death, the vampire morphed from monster to an **immortal** hero.

Cast members of *The Twilight Saga: Breaking Dawn* portray immortal heroes who look like normal humans.

## FAST FACT

Today, the vampire myth continues to teach us what we struggle to understand. Perhaps more important than overcoming illness and death, the vampire may help us to overcome our fear of the unknown.

# INFECTIOUS
## FEARS

## SCARED TO DEATH

In the beginning, there was life. People filled this life with many remarkable activities, accomplishments, and experiences. Sometimes, people fell ill. Why? Was it a curse? A demon spirit bullying their body and soul?

Perform the right ritual, and the curse might go away. Call upon the wisest **shaman** or healer, and they might successfully drive the demon out. When the rituals and shamans failed, death triumphed. But what was death? The body rotted away, but what of the soul? Was that unique personality a spirit, and if so, where did it go when the body was gone?

A shaman in Ecuador performs a healing ceremony that involves drinking a tea made from the ayahuasca plant. Found in the rainforest, the hallucinatory plant is considered to have medicinal properties.

# MODERN MARVELS

It is no easy task to imagine how the earliest peoples perceived the world around them. How can we *unknow* all that we now know about physics, chemistry, and biology? From our modern standpoint, we know that illnesses are triggered by **microbes**. Billions upon billions of microscopic bacteria populate Earth. Most of them are helpful, like the ones living in our digestive tracts that help us digest food. Others are harmful and make us sick. Viruses are another cause of illness and death in people and animals.

Flu viruses (shown here magnified many times) are even smaller than bacteria.

## FAST FACT

To make yogurt, simply add bacteria such as *Lactobacillus bulgaricus* and *Streptococcus thermophilus* to fresh milk warmed to a temperature of about 110°F (43°C). Let set for at least 4 hours, then chill. Yum!

# SEEING IS BELIEVING

Tens of thousands of years ago, people did not know about bacteria and viruses. As a result, they could not explain disease and death. Myths arose as people tried to explain what they saw. One common observation was the way in which plagues spread across entire villages, regions, or countries. When these tragedies occurred, people believed it was a curse from the heavens or the work of demons. They knew nothing of how germs spread through physical contact, bodily fluids, or even just floating through the air on a sneeze.

## AFTERLIFE

In the past, anyone who became sick and died was buried quickly to keep any infection from spreading. And yet, soon after the death, the same illness might attack family members or neighbors. People then did not know that most diseases develop slowly after contact, often without immediate symptoms or signs of illness. So they concluded there was only one way that an illness could be transmitted after death. The corpse would have to become reanimated, climb out of its grave, and attack the living.

In olden times, people believed the dead could come back to life and crawl out of the grave.

# BLOODY FEAST

Another factor contributing to the belief in vampires came not from the germs that couldn't be seen, but from things that could be seen all too clearly. In the twelfth century, historian William of Newburgh compiled a gigantic history book of the happenings in England from 1066 to 1198. Working like a modern-day investigative reporter, Newburgh filled his *Historia Rerum Anglicarum* ("history of English affairs") with accounts from many chroniclers and eyewitnesses who all testified that corpses really were turning into vampires—rising from their graves and returning to feast on the blood of the living.

Some fans of the TV series *True Blood* love the vampire characters because they often drink synthetic blood made in a laboratory. Here, Stephen Moyer, Anna Paquin, and Alexander Skarsgård arrive at the Hollywood premiere in 2010.

The heart was considered the most vital organ for life. To remove the heart would ensure that a corpse could not come alive again.

## GRIM BROTHERS

According to legend, two brothers teamed up to rid a European village of a vampire who walked the streets at night accompanied by a pack of vicious dogs. Wherever it went, the walking corpse spread disease.

First, the brothers dug up the grave and found the corpse with red-stained mouth and lips, proof that it must have been biting victims to drink their blood. They also found that rather than wasting away and shrinking as all rotting bodies should, this one was plump—**bloated** like a leech, in fact! The brothers decided to rip out the corpse's accursed heart and put an end to its fiendish feasting. They went on to whack the body with a blunt spade and remove the heart. Then they burned the corpse to a crisp. Soon after they did this, the plague lifted from their town.

## ROTTEN DEAL

Similar reports of "undead" corpses cropped up elsewhere in Europe. Some even noted that the fingernails and teeth of the corpses had grown—more proof that the body was undead.

Actually, what the vampire hunters observed were the natural signs of typical decomposition. Bacteria in a corpse consume tissues and give off gases, causing the body to bloat. The shrinking of skin and gums causes the illusion that nails and teeth have grown.

## BURIED ALIVE

Before stethoscopes could hear the heart, and before **electrocardiography** could translate a living heartbeat into a steady beep, determining death was difficult. Corpses were buried quickly—sometimes too quickly. Some people were just unconscious when buried. Imagine waking up covered in dirt. The lucky ones were able to climb out!

Witnesses who claimed to see people crawl out of their graves may have actually seen just that.

The rabies virus was thought to transform people into werewolves and vampires.

## RABIES

Vampire scares tended to correspond with outbreaks of disease. Rabies epidemics triggered hysteria over werewolves and vampires because rabies is transmitted through biting—a favorite activity of both monsters. It is not a coincidence that the animals most commonly associated with spreading rabies—wolves, dogs, and bats—are the same animals people once thought vampires changed into.

The rabies virus attacks the nervous system. It drives victims mad with thirst, but drinking water causes choking. Breathing becomes difficult, so sufferers clench their teeth and roll back their lips—and look like a vampire gnashing its fangs.

# BIT BY BIT

## FATAL KNOWLEDGE

Death presents a slew of difficult challenges for the living. Losing a loved one leads to shock, grief, and sometimes anger. As a biological process, death is both mystifying and revolting. Limbs may jerk or twitch as muscles decompose. In some cases, the epidermis, or top layer of the skin, slides completely off the body like a glove.

Microbial gases escape from body openings as groans or moans. The sounds of escaping gases can sometimes be mistaken for breathing.

The corpse is an eerily still object — until it is not!

### FAST FACT

Most of the world's religions assume that an afterlife exists, though what it looks like, and what spirits do there, varies widely. Most cultures seem to agree that mistreating a **cadaver** hinders its spirit's passage into the afterlife, resulting in extremely unpleasant consequences.

# FORGET-ME-NOT

As far back as the second century BC, the Chinese followed strict and complicated funeral rites in order to pave a spirit's way into heaven. They wove ropes and tied intricate knots around dead bodies, securing them to the inside of the coffin. The slightest error meant that the spirit would fail to reach its final destination. Restless or vengeful, the spirit would reanimate the body and escape the grave in order to hunt down and punish the living. This monster, a *jiang shi*, sustained itself on a diet of blood sucked from the living.

## TERRACOTTA ARMY

During the late third century BC, the first emperor of China, Qin Shi Huang, had an army of 9,000 **terracotta** figures buried in his tomb. The warriors were meant to protect the emperor from *jiang shi* in his afterlife.

The Terracotta Army was uncovered in March 1974 by farmers digging a well in Xi'an, China. It is now a UNESCO World Heritage site.

## FAST FACT

The practice of burying the dead may date back 350,000 years. Today, especially in large cities in China, the dead are often cremated rather than buried.

14

# BURIED SECRETS

The Chinese are not unique when it comes to intricate and strict burial practices. Archaeologists have found complex burial rituals around the world dating back tens of thousands of years. Not only that, researchers find that humankind has shared a common fear of **revenants** returning from the dead. This fear resulted in burial practices designed to keep the body in its grave. Heavy boulders, or what we call tombstones, are just one example.

## MASCHALISMOS

The ancient Greeks practiced *maschalismos*, or mutilation of the cadaver, to prevent the dead from returning to life. Vital organs including the brain, heart, and liver were removed. The Slavic peoples of Eastern Europe had a similar zero-tolerance policy on revenants. They bound the corpse, slit the muscles and tendons, cut off limbs, and drove a stake or cross through the heart. Lastly, a lump of dirt was jammed into the mouth to keep the revenant cadaver from biting anyone.

Driving a stake through the heart ensured that a corpse was truly dead.

# BABIES BEWARE!

In many countries, childbirth was a source of danger and deep fear. Both mothers and babies often died in the process. Unaware of the causes of disease, people developed myths about female vampires whose favorite snack happened to be pregnant mothers or their newborn babies.

## LANGSUYARS

In old Malaysian tales, women who died during childbirth returned as *langsuyars*, or vampires. Some stories describe a beautiful vampire with flowing, ankle-length hair. Others describe a floating head with **entrails** hanging to the ground. Regardless of their appearance, *langsuyars* preyed on the blood of newborns. Similarly, the Inuit people living east of Hudson Bay in Canada believed that the *tammatuyuq* preyed upon infants so that it could insert a needle into their skulls and extract their life force.

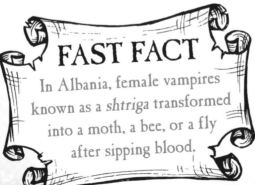

Notice the long hair and nails on this *langsuyar* figurine.

## FAST FACT

In Albania, female vampires known as a *shtriga* transformed into a moth, a bee, or a fly after sipping blood.

# SANGUINE SISTERS

Hebrew mothers-to-be used to dread Lilith, the first wife of Adam in the Garden of Eden. Lilith was neither docile nor obedient. She made friends with many demons and took up the disturbing hobby of stealing babies to drink their blood. In ancient Greek mythology, Lamia is Lilith's closest cousin. According to legend, Lamia made an enemy of Hera, the wife of the god Zeus. Vengeful Hera killed all of Lamia's children and transformed the woman into a blood-hungry demon who hunted children and babies.

Lilith is the vampire of ancient Hebrew legends.

# HOCUS POCUS, ABRA-CADAVER

In the folklore of many countries, vampires are created by witchcraft. Among the Maliseet Passamaquoddy tribes in the northeastern United States, witches turn corpses into flesh-hungry blood fiends called *kiwahkw*. If a *kiwahkw* can devour three people, then it will transform into a fearsome ice giant.

In African folklore, the creatures with vampiric powers are the witches themselves. The *obayifo*, a monstrous witch known among the Ashanti of West Africa, can leave its body behind at night and travel through the air as a ball of light on a gruesome quest for blood. With the slave trade, vampiric witch legends spread to the American colonies where slaves worked on plantations. As a result, the *obayifo* became known as the *asema* of Suriname and the *sukyuan* of Trinidad.

To this day, witches evoke fear.

# GARDEN OF EVIL

Elsewhere in the world, there are even stranger vampires to avoid. Roaming the lonely deserts of the Southwestern US or the jagged mountain ranges of Mexico, for example, runs the high risk of a fatal encounter with the *chupacabra*. The word literally means "goat-sucker," but the vampiric beast has been known to attack all sorts of animals.

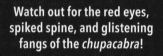

Watch out for the red eyes, spiked spine, and glistening fangs of the *chupacabra*!

And if you are ever in the tropical jungles of the Philippines, the Bagobo Malay people will warn you to avoid the *buso*. These tall, thin demons have a single eye and a gross mouth pronged with two large fangs. A *buso* may prefer to feast on rotting carcasses, but that has never stopped it from occasionally luring live victims to a very unpleasant death.

It's hard to miss the fangs on the *layak*, a vampire in Balinese lore.

19

# THAT SUCKS!

The Tschwi and Ashanti people of West Africa have warned children and travelers to beware lingering under certain trees, especially the banyan, which dangles long aerial roots from its branches. According to legend, this is where the *sasabonsam* dwells. It uses its long legs, often mistaken for hanging roots or vines, to snatch up unwary victims. It will suck out their blood or bathe in it. The few survivors of such attacks report that the *sasabonsam* has straight hair and bloodshot eyes.

Likewise, the indigenous peoples of Australia once told horrifying tales of the *yara-ma-yha-who*, a four-foot-tall red man with a large head, big mouth, and fingers and toes resembling the suckers of an octopus. *Yara-ma-yha-who* hid in tall trees and jumped down on children who wandered away from their parents. Either the little red man swallowed them whole, or he sucked their blood through his fingers and toes.

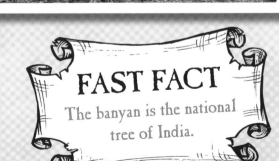

A banyan tree starts out as a fig plant. The banyan's seeds can get stuck in a crack of another tree, germinate, and then grow on that host tree.

## FAST FACT
The banyan is the national tree of India.

20

# BLOOD
## TIES

## THE RED ZONE

Despite the languages, borders, and customs that separate humanity into various groups, people across the globe still manage to find common explanations for common phenomena. For instance, the world usually agrees that vampires crave blood.

Throughout human existence, blood has been one of the great magical and mystical elements. Many of the earliest civilizations, including the Phoenicians, Persians, Egyptians, and Hebrews, wove blood into their creation myths. Wherever there was life, there had to be blood. Warriors painted it on their bodies. Tribal shamans and Druid priests splattered it on temple walls for protection or to attract certain spirits.

## IN LIVING COLOR

Mammals, including humans, bleed red. That is because hemoglobin, the protein inside red blood cells, contains reddish iron. Iron binds to oxygen much as static sticks socks together in the dryer. In other creatures, different metals bind with oxygen, creating other blood colors such as blue, purple, pink, yellow, orange, or green!

The horseshoe crab has blue blood.

21

# THICKER THAN WATER

As many as 60,000 miles of blood vessels curve, twist, and bundle around your entire body! Blood seems magical not only because it links us to life, but also because of its many strange behaviors. It beads out of small cuts, but gushes dark, hot, and sticky from deep wounds. It visibly steams in cold air. It smells of sour salt but tastes like acidic metal. It clots into grisly scabs. If left to settle in a vial, a sample of blood gradually separates into four layers—dark clot on bottom, then a vivid red fluid, then a whitish layer and finally, yellow **serum** on top.

We have the technology to separate blood into its many microscopic components, such as red and white blood cells, platelets, and plasma. We also know that blood is essential for transporting nutrients, oxygen, and chemical signals within the body, and for fighting off infections.

No matter what they look like, vampires cannot live long without blood.

# BLOODTHIRSTY

The vampire's lust for blood makes it one of the most terrifying mythical creatures. While the Roman gladiators drank blood to boost their bravery, Christianity, Judaism, and Islam **ostracized** people who drink blood. Similarly, the Alaskan Inuit exiled the dreaded *Iraaq*, a child vampire that drained its parents' blood when they neglected to give it ice cream at an annual festival. The Tukano people of the Amazon forest fled from the *boraro*, a tall, pale humanoid bloodsucker with a hairy chest and no knee joints. Similarly, the Tamil mythology of India warned of the *pey*, a kind of ghoul with shaggy hair. It preferred to skulk around battlefields where it could drink from soldiers' wounds.

Vampires would have a hard time getting their favorite drink without fangs. The *auyainá*, which was once believed to hunt the Tupari people of Brazil, is said to have had fangs the size of tusks. Likewise, in Eastern European and Russian folklore, Baba Yaga was a hideous ogress vampire whose fangs were rumored to be made of stone or knife blades!

Baba Yaga lives in a hut that stands on chicken legs deep in the forest. If you're not good, Baba Yaga will get you!

## FAST FACT

A researcher in Transylvania created an artificial blood perfect for humans. It comes from the purple blood found in many underwater worms. It is thought to be safer than donated blood because it is 100 percent germ- and disease-free!

23

# VAMPIRE BATS

Another reputed feature of the vampire is its ability to turn into a bat. Bats play a vital role in pollinating plants and eating insects that would otherwise bother people. Unfortunately, the bat has become associated with evil spirits, perhaps because it is nocturnal—active after dark. Owls, rats, and other nighttime hunters have gained a similar reputation.

Many people think the vampire bat is terrifying even though it is only about the size of a teacup and weighs as much as two slices of bread.

## THE TOOTH, AND NOTHING BUT THE TOOTH

Of the 1,200 species of bats, only three survive on blood. These vampire bats attack victims while they sleep. They use their razor-sharp teeth to make painless incisions along juicy body parts, such as fingertips and toes. However, it takes vampire bats about half an hour to drink a single ounce of blood.

# BODY OF EVIDENCE

The skeletal body of a bat bears a spooky resemblance to the human skeleton. As a result, many people believed that vampires transformed themselves into bats. The Maya, a people who once lived in what is now Central America, worshipped a bat deity known as Camazotz, the god of caves.

In surviving Mayan artwork, Camazotz is depicted as part man and part bat.

The link between bats and vampires all but solidified when Spanish conquistadors discovered vampire bats living in South America in the 1600s. Whereas most bats eat plants and bugs, a few species drink blood.

## FAST FACT

The saliva of vampire bats contains an anticoagulant — something that prevents blood from clotting. It was first named *draculin*, after the title character in Bram Stoker's gothic novel, *Dracula*.

# SMELLS LIKE SUCCESS

It is no coincidence that garlic crops up as an essential vampire repellent. The ancient Egyptians believed that garlic deterred ghosts. In parts of Asia, garlic smeared over the body shielded against spells cast by witches or wizards. But vampires found garlic especially repulsive. In Romania in the 1600s, the best advice for fending off vampires was to hang garlic over your entire house.

Before modern **embalming** methods, bulbs of pungent garlic were used to mask the smell of decaying corpses during burial rituals. As an added bonus, they might also keep the revenant corpse from rising to suck blood.

Good for the immune system and essential to many cuisines, garlic has been a special plant for thousands of years.

## RAISE THE STAKES

If garlic failed to ward off a vampire, then the next step would be to kill the creature. Driving a stake through the heart was considered a reliable method around the world. A stake served two purposes. First, it pinned the wandering vampire to the ground. Once staked, the corpse could not prowl at night. Second, a stake through the heart was the only way to make the undead very dead. According to most African folklore, vampires required two stakes: one through the heart and one to nail the tongue to the chin. This would prevent the undead from uttering spells and curses.

## MAKE NO MIS-STAKE

Some cultures called for a wooden stake, particularly of ash, juniper, or hawthorn. Others claimed an iron stake was the only reliable weapon. According to Russian legends, the material of the stake didn't matter so much as driving it through the vampire's heart in a single blow.

Many different cultures believed that driving a stake through the heart would kill a vampire.

# FIRED UP

When permanently snuffing out a vampire's reign of terror, the only thing more effective than a stake through the heart was fire. In Bulgaria, Romania, Russia, and Poland, fire was the ultimate weapon of mass vampire destruction. The Hebrew god once appeared in the form of a burning bush and often used fire to punish people, destroy cities, and cleanse the Earth. Fire blazes as a powerful symbol across human cultures because it is one of the greatest technological innovations of our species. But with so many effective ways to recognize and eliminate vampires, how does the myth manage to survive and thrive?

With fire, we can be warm, have light, and barbeque!

## FAST FACT

In Greek mythology, Prometheus stole fire from the gods and shared it with humankind.

# GOING VIRAL

If we think of the vampire myth as a pot of soup on the stove, simmering on a fire of mysterious diseases, then it would have boiled over in the 1300s when the bubonic plague ravaged Europe, killing millions of people! Throughout the next few centuries, as Europe's most powerful countries sought to colonize the world, travel and trade spread typhoid, diphtheria, cholera, and other dreaded diseases.

Simultaneously, the vampire myth went viral. In the 1700s, wild stories from Hungary, Bulgaria, and Prussia (today, much of Germany, Lithuania, Latvia, and Estonia) made headlines in newspapers across Europe. By 1800, however, a significant shift had occurred.

The bubonic plague (1347–1353) was believed to cause vampirism. Doctors wore masks, the beaks stuffed with aromatics to cover the stench of death and decay.

# TURNING POINT

## DEEP CUTS

The Age of Enlightenment in the 1700s ushered in an era when science displaced superstition. The study of gross anatomy—carefully cutting open a cadaver to study the internal systems of veins, organs, and bones—enabled surgeons to understand how the human body worked. By the 1800s, technological innovations such as the stethoscope and microscope were revolutionizing medicine. Doctors could now see the microbes that destroyed human tissue. Joseph Lister, a British surgeon, invented the first antibacterial agents, while Florence Nightingale, a British nurse, fought to improve nursing standards in all hospitals.

Once science had surgically removed the inexplicable from the world, the result for vampires was devastating. The mythical **scapegoat** for diseases was no more—and the myth of the vampire nearly died with it.

## LEECHES

Leeches, nature's vampires, have been used in medicine for over 2,500 years. Today they are still used in delicate surgeries, such as those on the tiny veins of our ears. They also help tissue to mend after surgery on fingers and toes.

Leeches are also used in modern medicine to prevent clots.

# LOUIS PASTEUR

While modern medicine crushed many infectious diseases, rabies continued to elude successful treatment. Nearly all who were infected died. Born in 1822, Louis Pasteur was nine years old when a rabies outbreak struck his town in France. He witnessed how the disease transformed victims into snarling monsters—lips rolled back and teeth clenched like a vampire's.

Later in life as a physician, Pasteur was able to develop a **vaccine** against rabies. His students and colleagues used his methods to conquer some of the world's worst diseases.

Pasteur (above) developed the rabies vaccine and saved the lives of many victims.

## FAST FACT

Edward Jenner, an English physician, was one of Pasteur's heroes. Years before the rabies vaccine, Jenner created a vaccine to prevent the deadly disease of smallpox.

31

# POLIDORI'S "VAMPYRE"

As science gained more ground, humankind no longer seemed in need of its monster myths. The old tales might have faded away had not four friends met in 1816 to tell some ghost stories.

George Gordon—better known as the poet Lord Byron—together with his personal physician Dr. John Polidori, Percy Bysshe Shelley, and Mary Wollstonecraft Godwin, gathered for a few weeks of summer fun at a ritzy lake house in Switzerland. They were all wealthy, well-known writers. One night, Byron challenged everyone to write the scariest story ever told. Polidori wrote a creepy tale entitled "The Vampyre," which revived the myth and ensured its eternal survival.

Some people thought Lord Byron (shown here) wrote "The Vampyre," but both Byron and Polidori confirmed that Polidori was the author.

## FAST FACT

Mary Godwin, who later married Percy Shelley, eventually published her chilling tale, Frankenstein: or, the Modern Prometheus. It became a worldwide sensation that helped kick off today's fascination with zombies.

# DRACULA RISING

Unlike all the old mythical vampires, Polidori's character, Lord Ruthven, was a suave, rich British gentleman. This vampire was... romantic! In 1897, the Irish writer Abraham (Bram) Stoker repeated Polidori's formula in his novel Dracula. Stoker's villain, Count Dracula, was also wealthy and charming. He traveled from Transylvania to the seaside town of Whitby, England, where he sought new victims to sustain his undead existence.

Stoker carefully researched many vampire folktales to craft his masterpiece. He may have based his villain on a fifteenth-century nobleman named Vlad Dracula, who ruled Wallachia, now part of Romania.

Bram Stoker is still famous in Dublin, Ireland, his birthplace.

DUBLIN AND EAST TOURISM

BRAM STOKER
1847 – 1912

THEATRE MANAGER

AUTHOR OF DRACULA

LIVED HERE

# THE REAL DRACULA

Vlad Dracula learned at a young age to trust no one. His own father sent the boy and his older brother to live as hostages. Throughout the Middle Ages, dueling leaders often sent relatives as hostages in order to ensure peaceful relations between their territories. But little Vlad did not like being a hostage and grew up suspicious of everyone.

It was a dangerous and violent time. When he was a teenager, the royal Hungarian families murdered Vlad's father and brother. Vlad vowed to claim his throne and spent the rest of his life trying to avenge his father's death. He battled the Turks and the Hungarians. To achieve his ruthless goals, he made friends of enemies, and enemies of friends.

## FAST FACT

Vlad Dracula liked to sit and watch his victims die while he ate. Although he didn't suck blood as the fictitious count did, some sources say he dipped his bread in his victims' blood.

Vlad was a fierce warrior who developed a reputation for cruelty to his enemies.

Today, Bran Castle is a popular museum and landmark.

## DRACULA'S CASTLE

In his novel *Dracula*, Bram Stoker may have chosen Bran Castle as the model for his evil vampire's spooky home. Bran Castle was one of several castles in Wallachia that Vlad and his father might have used to stage attacks or seek refuge after a defeat.

Christian Crusaders built the stone castle in 1211 high atop a mountain. At 2,500 feet, Bran Castle loomed high above the gorge below, allowing its knights to easily spot invading Turks. Besides being a sort of watchtower, the castle played many roles in its lifetime. In 1920, it became the summer residence of the kings of Romania. During World War II, it functioned as a hospital to treat injured soldiers. On June 1, 2009, the castle reverted back to its legal royal heirs.

## VLAD THE IMPALER

In his quest for vengeance, Vlad Dracula acquired a bloody reputation. According to some estimates, Vlad killed 40,000 people. He impaled most victims on tall stakes, earning him the nickname Vlad Tepes, meaning Vlad the Impaler.

## ORDER OF THE DRAGON

Though the word *dracul* meant "devil," the name Dracula originally meant "dragon." In 1431, Vlad was inducted into the Order of the Dragon, a military-religious order created in 1408 by King Sigismund of Hungary. Recruits were required to defend Christianity against its enemies, such as the Ottoman Turks. Membership in this order was considered a great honor.

This is the symbol for the Order of the Dragon. The order was fashioned after those of the Crusades.

# CRUEL BEYOND BELIEF

Some believe that Vlad learned the art of impaling from his captors as a child hostage. When he captured an enemy or caught his own people stealing, he would impale them by carefully sliding a wooden stick through the body without hitting any vital organs. That would ensure that the victim would die a slow and painful death. Then the victim would be displayed in public. This punishment served as a warning not to defy him.

Displaying impaled victims in public served as a warning against defying Vlad's rule. This impalement scene is reenacted at a castle on Mount Cetatea in Romania.

## FAST FACT

Legend has it that Vlad had mugs made of gold placed at all the fountains in his kingdom. He ordered that only those mugs could be used to drink the water. The people were so afraid of him that none of the mugs were ever stolen!

# HEARTH THROBS

Bram Stoker's *Dracula* terrified worldwide audiences who felt the globe had become smaller thanks to technological innovations such as the steam locomotive and the electric telegraph. His count used technology to his advantage, always outwitting the heroes. He also stumped physicians, who were thought to rule the very forces of nature with their amazing cures.

## REVAMP OR PREVAMP?

Stoker's *Dracula* cemented many of the modern iconic traits of a vampire, including white fangs, black suits and capes, failing to cast a reflection in mirrors, susceptibility to holy water, and an aversion to crucifixes.

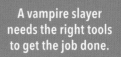

A vampire slayer needs the right tools to get the job done.

# BELA LUGOSI

In the 1931 film *Dracula*, renowned stage actor Bela Lugosi starred as the count whom everyone recognizes to this day. Wearing a tuxedo and black cape, his black hair slicked down with a distinct V-shaped widow's peak crowning his forehead, Lugosi became the ultimate vampire for generations to come.

Stoker's villain allowed the vampire myth to thrive across hundreds of books, movies, comic books, and games. US author Anne Rice continued the tradition in her bestselling series *The Vampire Chronicles*, popular from the 1970s to today. Young adult fiction writer Stephanie Meyer stoked the mythical fires further with her release of the *Twilight* series (2005–2008). Both the books and their film adaptations have attracted millions of fans.

Bela Lugosi as

# DRACULA

Bela Lugosi is still considered the definitive Count Dracula.

## FAST FACT

*Interview with the Vampire* is the 1976 novel by Anne Rice that became the first of *The Vampire Chronicles*. In 1994, the book was made into a blockbuster movie that revived interest in the vampire myth.

## NOSFERATU

*Nosferatu* is the earliest surviving movie adaptation of Bram Stoker's *Dracula*. The word *nosferatu* derives from the Romanian word meaning "plague carrier." A German film director, F.W. Murnau, produced the movie in 1922 without Stoker's permission. Murnau changed all the character names for his "symphony of horror" and made his Dracula—renamed Graf Orlok—a long-fingered, bald-headed, pointy-eared, fanged monster played by the talented stage actor Max Schreck.

The director thought Schreck was so ugly that no makeup was required except for false ears and teeth. Schreck appeared for only 9 minutes of the 94-minute film. But ultimately, his performance succeeded in making one of the world's first horror flicks. *Nosferatu* was banned in Sweden for 50 years because it was considered too scary!

*Nosferatu* was the earliest portrayal of a vampire on the silver screen. It showed for the first time that a vampire could be killed by sunlight.

# I AM LEGEND

In 1935, US author Richard Matheson was barely nine when he saw the new horror film *Werewolf of London*. He never forgot how the bite scene literally scared him out of his seat. In 1954, he published what many consider one of the scariest vampire novels of all time—*I Am Legend*.

*I Am Legend* did away with romance. The vampires were once again bloodthirsty, ruthless, and the result of worldwide plague. The book also mutated the vampire from an undead millionaire to a next-door neighbor. That is to say, vampires moved out of their castles and into the modern suburbs of Los Angeles.

## FAST FACT

In the 1960s, the ordinary, everyday vampire appeared in comedic sitcoms such as *The Munsters* and *The Addams Family*.

Will Smith starred in the 2007 film adaptation of *I Am Legend*. The filmmakers spent $5 million on one scene to destroy the Brooklyn Bridge in New York City.

# IMMORTAL BELOVED

In the late 1990s, a quirky TV series called *Buffy the Vampire Slayer* debuted. No one in the industry thought it would last, but fans clamored for more year after year. The show featured a powerful female heroine and several LGBT characters.

Today, vampires live on as celebrities and heroes. They are (and maybe always have been) outsiders seeking acceptance. The only difference is that we no longer wish to slay them. Instead, we want to be just like them—eternally beautiful and immortally immune from the inexplicable mysteries of disease and death.

The hit TV series *The Vampire Diaries* (2009–2017), based on the books by L.J. Smith, takes many cues from its predecessor, *Buffy the Vampire Slayer.* The cast is seen here at the 2010 Teen Choice Awards.

# TRUTH SERUM

Even before *Buffy*, people claiming to be real vampires formed secretive fan clubs and societies across many countries, perhaps in response to another hit TV show, *Dark Shadows* (1966–1971), which also featured vampires.

The craze was so intense that researchers began rigorous studies and investigations of these groups. Were there really people who needed to consume blood in order to survive? Perhaps they had an undiagnosed medical condition.

One researcher, Stephen Kaplan, formed the Vampire Research Center in New York in 1971. He met donors, people who allowed **alleged** vampires to drink their blood for a fee. He also interviewed people who lived as vampires—going about by night and consuming blood instead of food. According to Kaplan, vampire societies organized themselves into houses, clans, or **covens**.

Vampire societies for fans and "lifestylers" fell under fire when Rod Ferrell, a teenager obsessed with vampires, committed a heinous double murder in 1996.

# OUT IN THE OPEN

To this day, the Atlanta Vampire Alliance (AVA) is among the most visible and open vampire groups, reporting nearly 1,000 people living as vampires in 40 countries around the world. Similarly, the Voices of the Vampire Community (VVC) emerged in 2006 aiming to promote friendly relationships among vampire groups along with healthy, educational discussions of the alternative lifestyle. The VVC boasts a global membership from countries including Australia, Austria, Canada, France, Germany, Spain, the United Kingdom, and the United States.

Today, many people like to dress up as vampires for Halloween.

# VAMPIRE MYTHS ACROSS THE MAP

Here are some of the places where vampire myths originated.

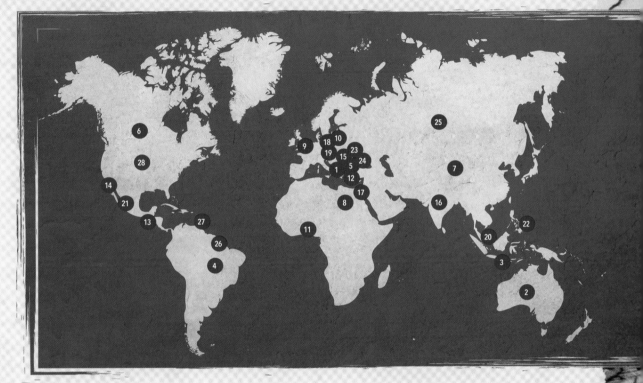

## MAP KEY

1. Albania
2. Australia
3. Bali
4. Brazil
5. Bulgaria
6. Canada
7. China
8. Egypt
9. England
10. Estonia

11. Ghana
12. Greece
13. Guatemala
14. Hollywood
15. Hungary
16. India
17. Israel
18. Latvia
19. Lithuania
20. Malaysia

21. Mexico
22. Philippines
23. Poland
24. Romania; Transylvania
25. Russia
26. Suriname
27. Trinidad and Tobago
28. United States

# GLOSSARY

**alleged** claimed but not proven

**bloat** to swell with water or gas

**cadaver** a dead body

**coven** a band of witches or vampires

**electrocardiography** recording electrical activity in the heart; sometimes called ECG or EKG

**embalming** preserving a corpse from decay

**entrails** internal organs

**immortal** able to live forever

**microbes** microorganisms, including bacteria, fungi, and viruses, that cause disease

**ostracize** to exclude someone from a society or group

**revenant** a person who has returned from the dead

**scapegoat** a person or thing that is blamed for something

**serum** blood plasma from which certain substances, such as those preventing clotting, have been removed

**shaman** a priest or priestess who uses magic to cure the sick, control natural events, or foretell the future

**terracotta** a reddish-brown baked clay used for pottery, statues, and building materials

**vaccine** a preparation of weakened infectious microbes that is given to prevent a particular disease

# FURTHER INFORMATION

## BOOKS

Burns, Charles. *Black Hole*. New York: Pantheon, 2008.

Dicce, "Count" Domenick. *You're a Vampire—That Sucks!: A Survival Guide*. New York: TargerPerigee, 2015.

Leitich Smith, Cynthia. *Feral Nights*. Somerville, Mass.: Candlewick, 2014.

National Geographic. *Louis Pasteur and Pasteurization*. Washington, DC: National Graphic Learning, 2010.

Small, David. *Stitches: A Memoir*. New York: W.W. Norton, 2010.

Telgemeier, Raina. *Ghosts*. Toronto: Scholastic Graphix, 2016.

## WEBSITES

Explore more vampire lore here!
**kids.britannica.com/students/article/vampire/601119**

Learn more about real-life vampire bats here!
**kids.nationalgeographic.com/animals/vampire-bat/#vampire-bat -ying-wings.jpg**

Read about Dracula's story at this cool site!
**encyclopedia.kids.net.au/page/dr/Dracula**

# INDEX